The Soups and Salads Cookbook

Illustrations by Lillian Langseth-Christensen

The Soups and Salads Cookbook

Lillian Langseth-Christensen and Carol Sturm Smith

Walker and Company   New York

Copyright © 1968 by Lillian Langseth-Christensen and Carol Sturm Smith

All rights reserved. No part of this book may be reproduced or transmitted in any form or by any means, electronic or mechanical, including photocopying, recording, or by an information storage and retrieval system, without permission in writing from the Publisher.

First published in the United States of America in 1968 by Walker and Company, a division of the Walker Publishing Company, Inc.

ISBN: 0-8027-2464-7
Library of Congress Catalog Card Number: 68–27558

Printed in the United States of America

This Walker Large Print edition published in 1984.

TABLE OF CONTENTS

HOW TO USE THE BOOK   7

SOUPS   8

SALADS   50

HOW TO USE THE BOOK

(1) Read the recipe through.

(2) Prepare and have ready all ingredients.

(3) Ingredients in parentheses are optional and can be omitted.

(4) Read general directions for washing and crisping salad greens and do this as soon as the greens are brought in from the market or garden.

(5) Prepare soup stocks in advance or use canned consommés and bouillons, or bouillon cubes or granules.

(6) Prepare salad dressings and mayonnaise in advance and store in refrigerator.

(7) Make menus around soups and salads. Combine with crisped breads or hot breads, wine, fruit and coffee or tea. When serving soup as a main course, increase quantities to fill soup bowls or large plates and allow for second helpings.

UNLESS OTHERWISE STATED, ALL RECIPES SERVE 6.

SOUPS

SOUP GARNISHES

(1) Whipped cream: Whip cream lightly, add a little salt to taste and continue to whip until stiff. Top hot soup with salted whipped cream after it has been served in cups or plates. The whipped cream may be sprinkled with paprika, cut chives or chopped parsley, toasted coconut, croutons or any garnish the recipe calls for. For gratinéed soups, sprinkle whipped cream with grated Parmesan cheese and brown for a minute under a hot broiler before serving.

(2) Hard-cooked eggs, riced or sliced, may be floated on the soup just before serving, as in Black Bean Soup, page 35.

(3) Bread croutons, fried or oven-dried, may be sprinkled over the soup or over whipped cream on the soup just before serving. Croutons may also be passed separately with the soup.

(4) Cut chives or chopped parsley may be sprinkled over the soup just before serving. See Vichyssoise, page 25.

(5) Grated Parmesan cheese is usually passed separately and sprinkled over minestrone and similar soups after they have been served.

(6) Sherry, wine or brandy is added to the soup after it is cooked and before it is served, or a small decanter is passed after the soup is served.

(7) Slices of lemon or lime are floated on some soups just before they are served.

(8) Dumplings, rice, noodles and pastas are usually boiled in the soup.

TOASTED CROUTONS

Preheat oven to 225°F.

(1) Cut 3–4-day-old bread into ½-inch slices, trim crusts and butter both sides of the bread. Cut into ½-inch cubes and spread on a baking sheet:
  ½ loaf unsliced bread
  ⅔ cup soft butter

(2) Bake, shaking frequently, until golden, about 40 minutes.

(3) Sprinkle warm croutons over hot cream soups and serve at once.

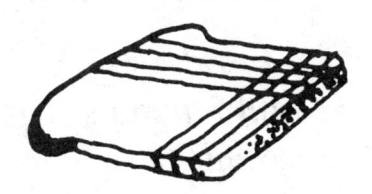

GARLIC CROUTONS

Follow directions for oven-dried croutons, adding 3 cloves garlic, crushed, to the soft butter before buttering the bread slices.

FRIED CROUTONS

Cut bread as for oven-dried croutons, fry the croutons in 2 tbs butter per cup of croutons, shaking the pan to brown the croutons evenly on all sides.

DUMPLINGS

(1) Sift into a bowl:
1 cup flour
1 tbs baking powder
½ tsp salt

(2) Cut in with a pastry blender or two knives:
1 tbs soft butter

(3) Stir in with blade of a knife:
6 tbs cold milk

(4) Shape with floured hands into dumplings the size of small marbles. Drop into simmering soup, cover and boil gently for 15 minutes:
3 qts stock or cream soup, simmering

(5) Sprinkle with:
3 tbs minced parsley

BEEF BOUILLON

Canned beef bouillon can be garnished in the following ways:

(1) Place 1 poached egg or 1 peeled 6-minute egg into each cup of hot beef bouillon. Sprinkle with chopped parsley.

(2) Add cooked noodles or pasta to hot beef bouillon. Garnish with minced parsley and pass grated Parmesan cheese separately.

(3) Combine ¾ beef bouillon and ¼ sherry. Serve very hot.

(4) In each cup of hot beef bouillon dissolve 1 envelope gelatin. Garnish with chopped parsley and lemon slices. A satisfying luncheon soup with few calories.

(5) For a hearty bouillon, heat 1 jar Italian ravioli, divide among 6 soup plates, add boiling hot bouillon and sprinkle with grated Parmesan cheese.

(6) Prepare any combination of vegetables, frozen, fresh or left over. Add hot bouillon and cook long enough to heat vegetables through.

(7) Dip 24 fingers of white or Italian bread into melted butter and bake in a 250°F oven until golden, about 30 minutes. Add hot bread fingers to hot bouillon and pass grated Parmesan cheese separately.

COLD CONSOMMÉS

Do not chill long enough to turn these soups into stiff jellies. They should be just barely firm and very cold. The following variations can be made with a base of canned jellied soups. (Jellied chicken consommé is clear and golden. Jellied madrilene is clear and tomato-colored. Jellied borsch is a deep beet-red color.)

(1)   Flavor jellied chicken consommé to taste with sherry or white port wine.

(2)   Flavor jellied madrilene to taste with red port wine, marsala or sherry.

(3)   Serve jellied madrilene or borsch in half cantaloupes and garnish with whipped sour cream, a sprig of dill and a slice or wedge of lime.

(4)   Serve jellied chicken consommé or madrilene in pitted half avocados. Garnish with whipped sour cream, sprigs of parsley and lemon wedges.

(5)   Pour jellied madrilene over 2 tsp red caviar and 1 tsp chopped parsley in each soup cup. Do not stir.

(6) Peel, seed and dice 3 medium tomatoes. Combine with ½ cucumber, peeled and sliced very thin; ¼ cup diced celery; and 1 tbs each finely chopped onion and parsley. Divide the mixture over 6 chilled soup cups and fill cups with jellied madrilene.

(7) Repeat variation 6, substituting 3 cooked beets, cut into matchsticks, for the tomatoes; fill cups with jellied borsch.

CHICKEN STOCK

(1) Bring to a boil in a large kettle:

8 cups water
1 carrot, scraped and sliced
1 onion, quartered
3 stalks celery, with leaves
¼ bay leaf
3 peppercorns
1 clove
salt to taste
1 curl lemon peel

(2) Brown lightly on all sides in a wide pan:

2 tbs butter
chicken fat from stewing fowl
1 4-lb stewing fowl, disjointed

(3) Add chicken and any fat from pan to kettle, cover and simmer until tender, about 2 hours. Cool and chill, remove fat and dice or grind chicken meat for garnish, sandwiches or salads. Strain stock through a triple cheesecloth wrung out in cold water; use stock as recipes require.

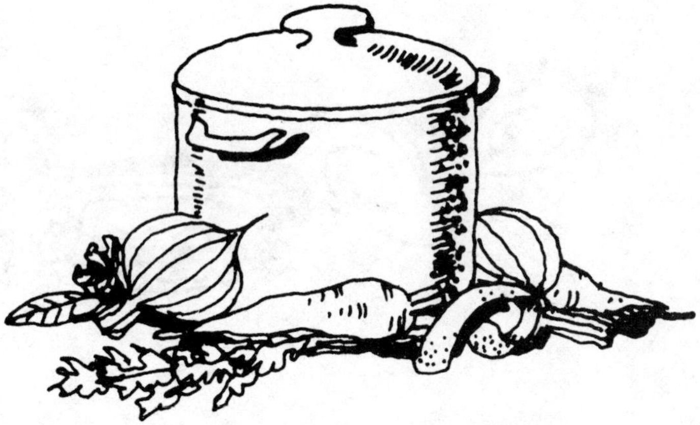

CREAM OF CHICKEN SOUP I

(1) In the top of a double boiler, over simmering water, or in a heavy saucepan, melt:
    8 tbs (1 bar) butter

(2) Stir in with a wooden spoon until smooth and bubbly but not brown:
    9 tbs flour

(3) Add gradually, stirring constantly until smooth and thickened:
    1 cup scalded milk
    4 cups chicken consommé or stock

(4) Reduce heat and let soup simmer for at least 20 minutes, preferably longer. The longer it simmers, the smoother it will become.

(5) Add and simmer long enough to heat through:
    1 cup heavy cream
    salt and pepper to taste

(6) Serve garnished with any of the following:
    chopped parsley
    cut chives
    diced chicken
    fried or oven-dried croutons

CREAM OF CHICKEN SOUP II
(WITH SHRIMP AND ASPARAGUS)

(1) Melt in a saucepan:

    4 tbs butter

(2) Stir in:

    6 tbs flour

(3) Add gradually, stirring constantly, until soup is smooth and thickened, reduce heat and simmer, stirring occasionally, for 15 minutes:

    4 cups chicken stock or canned
    chicken consommé

(4) Beat in a small bowl:

    2 egg yolks
    1 cup heavy cream
    1 pinch cayenne pepper
    salt and pepper to taste
    ½ cup of the hot soup, Step 3

(5) Reduce heat under soup to low. When soup stops simmering, stir in yolk mixture, Step 4, and stir for 3 minutes. Do not boil.

(6) Serve soup in plates or cups and garnish each portion with:

    3 hot cooked shrimp
    3–4 cooked asparagus tips
    1 tsp minced parsley or chives

VARIATIONS: Garnish soup with:

(1) slivered blanched almonds and chopped watercress
(2) toasted bread croutons, riced chicken liver pâté and minced parsley
(3) 4 slices tongue, cut into julienne strips, and 2 hard-cooked eggs, riced
(4) 6 poached artichoke bottoms, diced
(5) cooked asparagus tips, diced chicken meat and chopped chervil
(6) cooked spinach leaves, cut in large pieces, not chopped, and diced cooked chicken

Chilled soup may be garnished with salted whipped cream covered with cold cooked green peas and finely chopped mint.

SENEGALAISE

(1)   Prepare and pour into a bowl:
  1 recipe Cream of Chicken Soup I, page 17

(2)   Ladle into a cup and stir until smooth:
  ½ cup of the hot soup
  2 tbs madras curry powder

(3)   Return curried soup to bowl and repeat until flavored with curry to taste. Chill soup for at least 2 hours.

(4)   Serve in plates or wide cups, garnished with salted whipped cream covered with:
  slivered cooked chicken meat
  ¾ cup shredded coconut* fried in:
  2 tbs butter

* Fry coconut over medium-low heat, stirring, until it starts to turn golden, take from heat and stir. Return to heat for a few seconds at a time until golden. Coconut burns quickly. Watch carefully and turn onto paper towels as soon as the color is right.

NEW ENGLAND CLAM CHOWDER

(1) Sauté until golden in a heavy soup kettle, about 5–7 minutes:
¼ cup salt pork, diced

(2) Add and simmer 10 minutes longer:
*4 oz shucked clams, chopped
2 onions, sliced
2 leeks, trimmed and sliced
3 potatoes, peeled and diced
1 bay leaf
salt and pepper to taste
2 cups clam juice
liquor from the clams
2 cups water*

(3) Melt butter in a heavy pan over low heat, stir in flour and gradually stir in scalded milk until smooth and thickened. Reduce heat and simmer until needed:
*3 tbs butter
4 tbs flour
1½ cups scalded milk
salt and pepper to taste*

(4) Stir cream soup, Step 3, into clam chowder until smooth. If preferred:
1 cup heated heavy cream may be added before serving

(5) Add to each serving:
1 tsp butter

MANHATTAN CLAM CHOWDER

(1) Cut into dice with a kitchen scissors and sauté in a heavy kettle until transparent, about 5 minutes:
6 slices chilled bacon

(2) Add and sauté 4 minutes, stirring:
2 onions, chopped

(3) Add and sauté 4 minutes longer, stirring:
2 carrots, scraped and diced
2 stalks celery, scraped and diced

(4) Add and simmer about 40 minutes:
1 cup clam juice
liquor from 2 cups shucked clams
1 1-lb can tomatoes
2 tbs chopped parsley
2 tbs thyme

1 bay leaf
salt and pepper to taste

(5) Add and simmer 15 minutes longer:
3 potatoes, peeled and diced

(6) Add, correct seasoning and simmer 10 minutes:
the 2 cups shucked clams, chopped

CLAM AND CHICKEN BROTH

(1) Heat to just under boiling in a heavy saucepan:
3 cups clam juice
3 cups clear chicken consommé

(2) Pour into cups and top with:
¾ cup heavy cream, whipped with salt to taste

(3) Sprinkle cream with:
2 tsp minced parsley

CLAM AND TOMATO BROTH

(1) Heat to just under boiling in a heavy saucepan:
3 cups clam juice
3 cups tomato juice

(2) Pour into cups and top with:
¾ cup heavy cream, whipped with salt to taste

(3) Top cream with:
2 lemons, sliced paper thin (use large center slices only)

CREAM OF LEEK AND POTATO SOUP
(HOT)

(1) Boil in salted water to cover for 14 minutes; drain:

4 potatoes, peeled and sliced

(2) Sauté lightly in a heavy kettle until limp and transparent, stirring frequently, about 12 minutes. Do not brown:

1 bar butter
1 bunch leeks, trimmed and cut across
into ½-inch slices
2 large onions, sliced and separated
into rings

(3) Add to kettle and continue cooking for 20 minutes:

the drained potatoes
3 cups chicken stock

(4) Press soup through a sieve or blend until smooth. Add and heat to just under boiling:

1 cup heavy cream
salt and pepper to taste

(5) Serve hot in wide plates, sprinkled with:

Garlic Croutons, page 11
chopped parsley to taste

VICHYSSOISE

(1) Prepare 1 recipe Cream of Leek and Potato Soup (hot), page 24, Steps 1 and 2. Add to kettle and continue to cook for 20 minutes:
the drained potatoes
2 cups strong chicken consommé

(2) Press soup through a sieve or blend until smooth with:
2 cups heavy cream
salt and (white) pepper to taste

(3) Chill and serve in chilled cups, garnished with:
2 tbs finely cut chives

GREEN TURTLE SOUP SIR JAMES

Combine, chill and serve in chilled cups:
2 19-oz cans green turtle soup
1¼ cups Madeira wine
¼ cup brandy
salt and pepper to taste

ABJY L'AMID

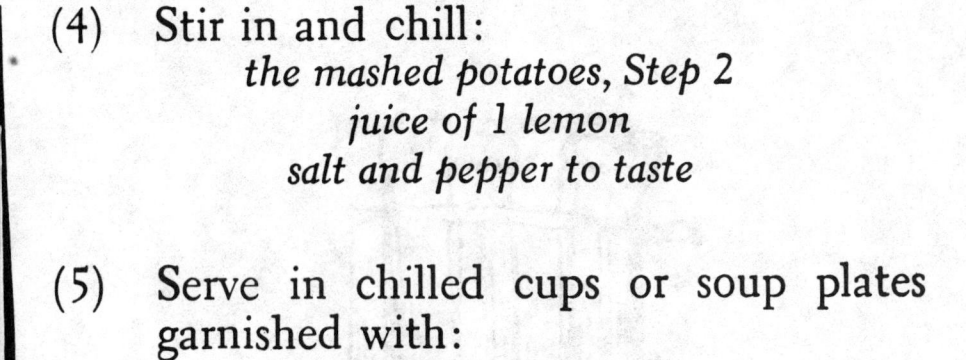

(1) Boil until soft in salted water to cover, about 15 minutes:
> 4 potatoes, peeled and sliced

(2) Mash or blend with:
> 1 cup warm milk
> salt and pepper to taste

(3) Melt butter in saucepan over low heat, stir in flour and gradually stir in milk and stock until smooth and thickened. Reduce heat and simmer 15 minutes, stirring occasionally:
> 4 tbs butter
> 4 tbs flour
> 1 cup warm milk
> 2 cups chicken stock or consommé

(4) Stir in and chill:
> the mashed potatoes, Step 2
> juice of 1 lemon
> salt and pepper to taste

(5) Serve in chilled cups or soup plates garnished with:
> 12 paper-thin lemon slices
> 3 tbs minced chervil or parsley

MUSHROOM SOUP

(1) Trim ends off stems and slice or chop caps and stems of:
   1 lb mushrooms

(2) Sauté onions in a heavy pan for 4 minutes, add mushrooms and cook, stirring, until they are dark and glossy, about 7 minutes:
   4 tbs butter
   1 onion, chopped
   the sliced or chopped mushrooms, Step 1

(3) Brown butter lightly in a heavy pan, stir in flour until golden, add stock and simmer, stirring occasionally, for 15 minutes:
   4 tbs butter
   5 tbs flour
   4 cups beef stock

(4) Add and stir until smooth and very hot:
   1 tbs beef extract
   ¼ cup warmed Madeira wine
   ½ cup heavy cream
   the mushroom and onion mixture, Step 2
   salt and pepper to taste

(5) Garnish with:
   ½ cup heavy cream, whipped
   3 tbs minced parsley

CHILLED CUCUMBER CREAM

(1) Simmer until transparent and tender, not brown, about 15 minutes, stirring frequently:
> 1 bar butter
> 4 cucumbers, sliced (peel if desired)
> 3 sprigs parsley, chopped
> 1 onion, sliced

(2) Add and press through sieve or blend until smooth:
> 2 cans jellied chicken consommé, at
> room temperature
> 1 cup heavy cream

(3) Chill. Serve with chilled whipped cream if desired. Garnish with:
> 2 tbs cut dill or chives

JELLIED BORSCH WITH WATERCRESS

(1) Chill until thickened, but not until solid:
> 1½-qt jar jellied borsch

(2) Divide among 6 chilled cups. Cover top with:
> 1 bunch watercress, leaves only, chopped

(3) In center of watercress topping, place:
> ¾ cup spiced beets, cut into matchsticks
> (about 2 tbs per cup)

(4) Pass separately:
> 1 cup chilled sour cream, whipped with:
> ½ tsp grated lemon rind
> ¼ tsp salt

SUMMER FRUIT SOUP

(1) Simmer until tender, about 35 minutes:
   1 lb dried apricots
   4 cups apple cider
   1 curl lemon peel

(2) Add and blend until smooth:
   juice of 1 lemon
   ¼ tsp ground cinnamon
   ¼ tsp ground cloves
   3 tbs sugar, or to taste

(3) Serve in chilled soup plates with a garnish of:
   ⅓ cup blanched almonds, shaved or chopped

GAZPACHO

Prepare and blend* in batches until smooth. Pour into chilled wide soup plates or cups. Add 1 ice cube to each serving:
   2 cloves garlic, crushed
   1 green pepper, seeded and roughly chopped
   2 cucumbers, roughly sliced
   2 onions, sliced
   6 ripe tomatoes, peeled
   1 slice whole-wheat bread
   ½ cup French Dressing I, page 88
   2 sprigs parsley
   2–3 cups tomato juice

*The vegetables may be chopped until liquefied if blender is not available.

MADRILENE OPORTO

(1) Simmer for 10 minutes:
   1 cup port wine
   ½ tsp saffron shreds

(2) Cool and pour into a bowl with:
   2 cans jellied madrilene, at room temperature

(3) Chill until soup is thickened but not solidified. Serve garnished with a sprinkling of:
   minced sage

KOLODNICK

(1) Prepare, chill and divide among 6 chilled cups:
   1 lb cold cooked shrimp
   3 hard-cooked eggs, sliced
   1 cucumber, peeled, seeded and diced
   2 slices smoked sturgeon, cut into strips

(2) Pour over the cups:
   4 cups chilled bouillon or 3 cans jellied chicken consommé, chilled until thickened but not stiff

CHILLED BUTTERMILK SOUP

(1) Combine in a large bowl and chill:
1 lb small cooked shrimp
1 cucumber, peeled, seeded and diced
1 tbs prepared mustard
1 tbs finely cut dill
1 tsp salt
¼ tsp sugar, or to taste

(2) Stir in and serve in iced cups:
1 qt chilled buttermilk
1 cup chilled sour cream, whipped

MALAKOFF SOUP
(HOT OR COLD)

(1) Combine and heat to boiling:
1 package Knorr's Leek and Potato Soup, prepared according to package directions
2 12-oz cans cream of tomato soup

(2) Simmer in the soup for 5 minutes:
1 cup stemmed spinach leaves, cut into strips

If preferred, chill the soup. Garnish with:
½ cup heavy cream, whipped

Sprinkle with:
chopped spinach leaves

31

CREAM OF GREEN PEA SOUP

(1) Boil until very soft in salted water to cover, about 15 minutes:

3 packages frozen green peas

(2) Press through a sieve or blend with:

1 cup beef bouillon

(3) Melt butter in a saucepan. Stir in flour and gradually add liquid, stirring until smooth and thickened. Reduce heat and simmer 15 minutes, stirring occasionally:

4 tbs butter
5 tbs flour
2½ cups milk

(4) Stir in, season and serve hot or cold:

the pureed peas
1 cup heavy cream
salt and pepper to taste

(5) Garnish with any of the following:

cold sliced tomatoes
chopped mint
Toasted Croutons, page 11
whipped cream and chopped chervil and parsley
whipped cream covered with cooked green peas
cooked shrimp and sherry

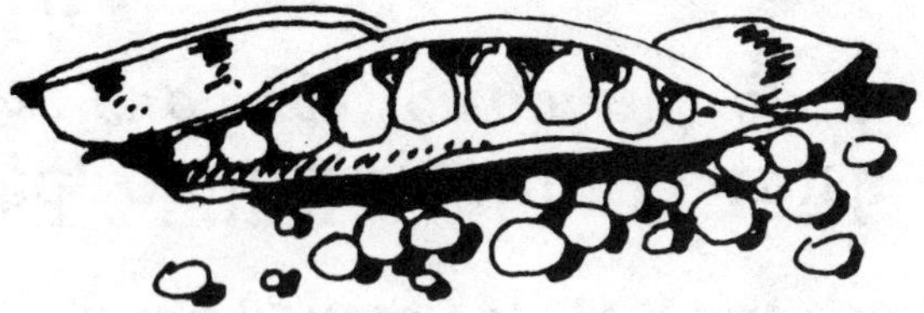

VARIATION: Cover soup with a heavy layer of whipped cream, sprinkle with Parmesan cheese and broil until cheese is browned, about 2 minutes. Keep broiler door open and watch carefully.

32

ONION SOUP

Preheat oven to 250°F.

(1) Slice, then cut each slice in half and toast in oven until parched and golden, about 40 minutes:
½ loaf French bread

(2) Sauté until golden in a heavy pan over medium heat:
½ cup butter
6 large onions, sliced, then divided into rings

(3) Transfer onions and butter to a soup kettle or casserole. Add and simmer:
4 cans strong beef bouillon
1 cup dry white wine
1 tbs Dijon mustard
2 tsp meat extract
celery salt and pepper to taste

(4) Add in order listed and serve:
¼ cup brandy
the toasted bread, Step 1
¾ cup grated Parmesan cheese

Bread and cheese may be passed separately, if preferred.

TOMATO SOUP

(1) Simmer until very soft, about 30 minutes, then blend or press through a sieve and set aside:

6 ripe tomatoes, quartered
2 onions, diced
5 peppercorns
thin peel of 1 lemon
1 pinch allspice
salt to taste
3 cups water or bouillon

(2) In a heavy saucepan, over low heat, melt butter, stir in flour and gradually stir in bouillon until thick and smooth:

2 tbs butter
3 tbs flour
1 cup bouillon

(3) Add sieved tomatoes and stir until smooth and hot. Add and bring to a boil.

2 tbs vinegar
1 tsp sugar
salt and pepper to taste

(4) Serve at once with Toasted Croutons, page 11.

34

BLACK BEAN SOUP
(CANNED)

(1) Heat according to directions on can:
    3 cans black bean soup

(2) Reduce heat to under simmer and add:
    ½ cup sherry

(3) Serve soup in cups and float on surface:
    3 hard-cooked eggs, sliced
    2 tbs minced parsley

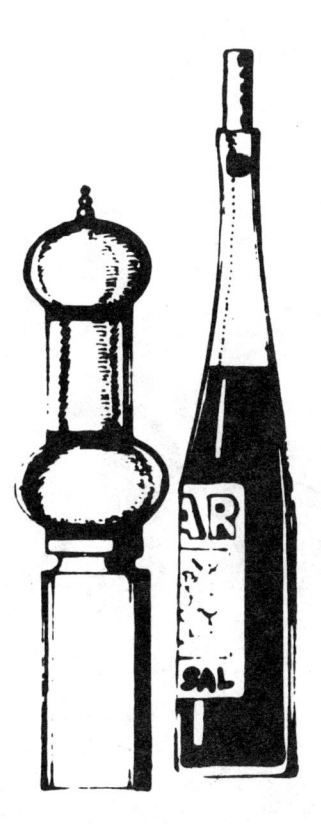

LENTIL SOUP I

(1)   Soak in water to cover for 8 hours or overnight:

1½ cups lentils

(2)   Pour lentils and the water in which they soaked into a soup kettle, add and simmer 1 hour:

1 ham bone*
7 cups water
2 onions, sliced thin
3 sprigs parsley, chopped
2 stalks celery, sliced thin
salt and pepper to taste
½ bay leaf
½ clove garlic, crushed

(3)   Remove ham bone and bay leaf and serve soup garnished with:

4 skinless frankfurters, heated and sliced

(If preferred, soup may be blended after ham bone is removed and before garnish is added.)

* If ham bone is not available, leftover ham, cut into dice or cubes, may be substituted.

LENTIL SOUP II

(1) Soak in water to cover for 8 hours or overnight:
2 cups lentils

(2) In a large heavy kettle, simmer but do not brown, for 7 minutes:
¼ lb (1 bar) butter
3 strips bacon, diced
3 onions, chopped
3 cloves garlic, crushed

(3) Add:
6–8 smoked pork chops, cut into single chops
1 bay leaf
1 tsp dried marjoram
8 cups water
salt and pepper to taste
the drained lentils

(4) Cover and simmer, stirring frequently, for 1 hour. Take out meat and cook soup 2 hours longer. Add a cup of water if soup becomes too thick. Add and cook until meat is heated:
2 tbs vinegar
the meat cut from the pork chops

(5) Serve each guest a wide plate of soup. If preferred, the whole chops can be returned to the soup and served with it.

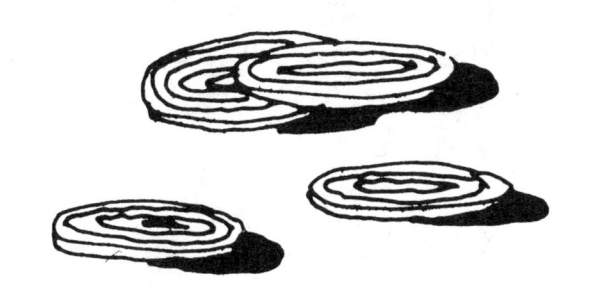

FISH CHOWDER

(1) Simmer uncovered for 2 hours in a heavy kettle until stock is reduced to 2½ cups; strain:

> 2 lbs fish trimmings
> 2 peppercorns
> ½ bay leaf
> 1 carrot, scraped and quartered
> 2 sprigs parsley
> salt to taste
> 4 cups water

(2) Simmer in a large kettle, stirring until onions are transparent, about 7 minutes:

> ½ cup butter
> 2 onions, chopped
> 1 bay leaf
> 2 tsp thyme

> 1 curl lemon peel
> 1½ lbs canned tomatoes
> 1–2 cups tomato juice

(3) Add and simmer 10 minutes longer:

> the strained fish stock, Step 1
> 4 potatoes, peeled and cubed
> salt and pepper to taste

(4) Add and simmer until potatoes are tender, about 7 minutes longer:

> 4 fish fillets, flounder or sole, cut into fingers
> juice of 1 lemon

(5) Serve very hot in large soup plates or bowls.

38

SALMON CHOWDER

(1) Follow recipe for Cream of Chicken Soup I, page 17, Steps 1 through 4, using:

> 6 tbs butter
> 6 tbs flour
> 2 cups scalded milk
> 2 cups chicken stock (or fish stock)
> salt and pepper to taste

(2) Add and puree soup through a sieve or with a blender:

> 1 7½-oz can salmon, broken into pieces
> ½ cup cream

(3) Return soup to heavy saucepan. Add and simmer until heated through:

> 1 package frozen green peas, cooked according to package instructions and drained
> 1 7½-oz can salmon, drained and broken into large chunks
> salt and pepper to taste
> 2 tbs sherry

(4) If soup is too thick, add:

> scalded milk to taste

STSCHY

(1) Simmer in a heavy kettle, stirring frequently:

¼ lb (1 bar) butter
1 small white cabbage, shredded
2 onions, sliced
½ pound lean beef, diced
2 leeks, trimmed and cut across into
½-inch slices
salt and pepper to taste
½ tsp caraway seeds

(2) When vegetables are limp and wilted, add and simmer until meat is tender, about 40 minutes:

2 cups beef stock, or more, to taste

(3) Take from heat and stir in slowly:

1½ cups sour cream, whipped with:

2 egg yolks
½ cup heavy cream

(4) Return soup to heat, but under no circumstances let it return to a boil. Stir over low warmth until smooth and thickened. Garnish with:

½ cucumber, peeled and thinly sliced
2 tbs chopped parsley

GULASCH SOUP

The Viennese traditionally eat Gulasch Soup on their way home or at home after they have danced all night.

(1) Brown in a heavy soup kettle, over medium heat, stirring, for about 7 minutes:
2 tbs butter
2 onions, sliced

(2) Add and simmer for 3–4 minutes:
1 lb stewing beef, cut into small pieces
½ lb fresh pork, cut into small pieces
2 large tomatoes, peeled and quartered

(3) Sprinkle over meat and stir until flour is browned and absorbed:
⅓ cup flour
2 tsp paprika
2 tsp salt

(4) Add and simmer, covered, until meat is almost tender, about 1–1½ hours:
10 cups water

(5) Add and simmer until potatoes are tender, about 25 minutes:
½ lb potatoes, peeled and cubed
½ tsp caraway seeds
¼ tsp pepper
salt to taste

(6) Cool and reheat in a double boiler or over low heat. Serve sprinkled with:
3 tbs chopped parsley or cut chives

ICED CHERRY SOUP

(1)   Drain juice from:
>   *1 1-lb can sour cherries*

(2)   Set cherries aside and reduce juice to 6 tbs by boiling over high heat. Combine:
>   *the 6 tbs reduced cherry juice*
>   *⅓ cup sherry*
>   *4 cups boiling beef bouillon*
>   *1 tsp dried chervil*

(3)   Cool soup slowly, pour through a strainer, add and chill:
>   *the drained cherries*

(4)   Serve in chilled cups with a few cherries in each serving.

TURKEY SOUP

(1) Bring to a boil in a large kettle. Cover and simmer for 2 to 2½ hours:
the cracked carcass and scraps of 1 turkey
2 celery stalks
2 carrots, scraped and quartered
1 onion, quartered
2 cloves
2 peppercorns
salt to taste
7 cups cold water

(2) Strain, return stock to rinsed kettle, add and reheat for 7 minutes:
1 cup cream
1 cup leftover giblet gravy if available
1 cup cubed turkey stuffing,* if available
2 tbs minced parsley

(3) Serve hot in wide cups or soup plates.

* Depending on the flavor of the stuffing, 6 boiled chestnuts or 12 small oysters may be added to the soup during Step 2.

CHILLED CARROT SOUP

(1) Simmer in a large kettle for 30 minutes, then blend or press through a sieve and set aside:

6 carrots, scraped and sliced thin
1 small onion, sliced
1 potato, peeled and diced
1 stalk celery, scraped and diced
3 cups stock or bouillon
salt to taste

(2) In a heavy saucepan, over low heat, melt butter, stir in flour and gradually stir in bouillon until thick and smooth:

3 tbs butter
4 tbs flour
1½ cups bouillon

(3) Add and chill:

the blended carrot soup
2 cups heavy cream
salt and pepper to taste

(4) Serve in chilled cups sprinkled with:

3 tbs cut chives

ICED SPINACH SOUP

(1) Follow recipe for Cream of Chicken Soup I, page 17, Steps 1 through 5, using:

6 tbs butter
6 tbs flour
2 cups scalded milk
2 cups chicken stock
1 cup heavy cream

(2) Simmer 10 minutes, then blend or pass through a sieve:

1 8-oz package washed spinach, stems and wilted leaves removed
½ cup water
salt to taste

(3) Combine and chill:

Cream of Chicken Soup
blended or pureed spinach

(4) Serve in chilled cups garnished with:

2 hard-cooked eggs, sliced

ASCONA MINESTRONE

(1) Soak overnight in water to cover:
 2 cups dried white beans

(2) Sauté very gently in a dutch oven or heavy kettle, stirring slowly for 7 minutes:
 ¼ cup diced bacon
 2 onions, chopped
 2 garlic cloves, minced
 2 tbs chopped parsley

(3) Add and stir 3–4 minutes longer:
 5–7 celery stalks, scraped and diced
 2 leeks, trimmed and sliced across
 2 carrots, scraped and sliced across

(4) Add, cover and simmer at least 1 hour:
 4 tomatoes, peeled, seeded and diced
 1 tsp rosemary, fresh or dried
 1 pinch thyme

 salt and pepper to taste
 7 cups boiling water

(5) Add and simmer 10 minutes longer:
 1 cup small shells or any preferred soup pasta
 1 cup frozen tiny green peas, thawed

(6) Serve hot in wide soup plates with:
 2–3 cups grated Parmesan cheese, passed separately

CHILLED CONSOMMÉ CARUSO

(1) Set into refrigerator until thickened but not stiffened:
    3 13-oz cans jellied chicken consommé

(2) Dip into boiling water for 10 seconds and peel:
    4 medium tomatoes

(3) Press out seeds and dice. Divide the tomato dice among 6 chilled cups. Sprinkle with:
    3 tbs minced parsley
    6 large stuffed olives, chopped

(4) Spoon the iced consommé over the parsley and olives, working carefully so that they stay at the bottom of the cup. Serve at once.

CONSOMMÉ DELICE

(1) Whip cream almost stiff, fold in:
    1 cup heavy cream
    salt to taste
    1 cup finely diced cold chicken meat
    3 tbs minced parsley

(2) Heat to boiling:
    6 cups chicken consommé

(3) Serve the hot consommé in 6 soup cups or plates and pass the whipped cream mixture separately.

TARATOR
ICED CUCUMBER SOUP

(1) Peel, seed and dice. Place in a large bowl:

3 medium cucumbers

(2) Add and chill:

4 containers yogurt
⅔ cup chopped walnuts
1 clove garlic, crushed
½ cup dry bread or zwieback crumbs
¼–⅓ cup French Dressing II, page 89

(3) Stir into the mixture, correct seasoning and serve in chilled soup cups:

½–1 cup chilled cream, more if soup is too thick

(4) Garnish with:

6 sprigs dill or watercress

CHICKEN AND LEMON SOUP

(1) Combine in a soup kettle and bring to a boil. Boil for 10 minutes:

6 cups chicken stock or consommé
½ cup rice

(2) Reduce heat to simmer. In the meantime, beat until smooth:

3 eggs
juice of 1½ lemons
1 cup of the simmering chicken stock

(3) Stir the egg mixture slowly back into the simmering soup. Simmer, stirring constantly for 3–4 minutes longer. Serve soup in heated plates with:

thin slices of the remaining ½ lemon

CREAM OF GREEN PEA SOUP WITH EGG
A MEAL IN ITSELF

Prepare 1 recipe Cream of Green Pea Soup, Steps 1 through 4, page 32.

(5) Divide the soup among 6 hot soup plates and garnish with:

6 freshly cooked and peeled 6-minute eggs, whole

3 tbs minced parsley

(6) Serve at once with:

6 slices whole wheat bread, toasted, buttered and cut into fingers

SALADS

PREPARING SALAD GREENS

(1) To prepare Boston, escarole, romaine, chicory, bibb, orchard, and other lettuce varieties: Remove broken or coarse outside leaves. Cut out stem with a sharp knife and separate leaves. Wash under running cold water and shake dry by hand or in a French wire lettuce basket. Place leaves in a large plastic bag, press out as much air as possible, seal and refrigerate until needed.

(2) Prepare iceberg and endive lettuces by removing outside leaves and trimming off enough of the stem or base so that leaves can be separated. Or remove outside leaves and base of endive stalks and slice across; or remove outside leaves and stem of iceberg lettuce and shred. Both varieties are so solid that they do not require washing.

(3) Prepare watercress and parsley by rinsing the bunch in cold running water. Cut off stems with their string or elastic band and spread leaves or sprigs on a kitchen towel. Discard wilted, yellow or scarred leaves and twigs and any remaining coarse stems. Place the leaves to be used in small plastic bags with the water that clings to them. Seal and refrigerate until needed.

ASPARAGUS SALAD

(1) Scrape, wash and cut off long stems, leaving 6-inch spears, and tie into bundles:

2 bunches asparagus

(2) Stand bundles up in 3 inches boiling, salted water and cover with a second saucepan. Steam asparagus until just tender, depending on age, 15–17 minutes. Drain and arrange log-stack fashion on an oblong platter. Chill. Before serving, drain any moisture from the platter and pour over asparagus:

½–¾ cup French Dressing II, page 89,
enough to seep through asparagus
but not to run over platter

(3) Garnish top of asparagus with:

3 hard-cooked eggs, sliced

(4) Surround with 12 toast rounds spread with:

1 cup chopped watercress
1 cup chopped ham
enough mayonnaise to bind

BEET SALAD

(1) Rinse and boil in salted water to cover until tender, 25–45 minutes, depending on age of beets:
>   2 bunches beets*

(2) Drain, scrape off skins and trim off root ends and stems. Slice warm beets into a bowl with a mechanical slicer or a sharp knife. Set aside.

(3) Simmer for 7 minutes; then pour over beets:
>   ½ cup tarragon vinegar
>   ½ cup water
>   3 cloves
>   1 bay leaf
>   2 peppercorns

(4) Cover and refrigerate until needed. Serve beets in their marinade. Add, just before serving:
>   2 tbs grated horseradish

(5) Serve with boiled beef, cold meats and in mixed salads.

* Do not cut off root ends or stems before boiling. Baby beets will require only 10–12 minutes' boiling time but are not as suitable in salad.

BROCCOLI SALAD

(1) Trim off long stems, simmer in salted water to cover for exactly 18 minutes, drain and chill:

2 bundles broccoli

(2) Arrange broccoli on lettuce leaves in a shallow salad bowl and pour over:

¾ cup French Dressing II, page 89

(3) Sprinkle over top:

1 roasted pimento, minced
2 tbs minced green pepper
2 tbs minced onion
2 tbs minced parsley

CAULIFLOWER SALAD

(1) Boil for 15 minutes, drain, chill and invert stem-side-up in a bowl, for 30 minutes:
    1 1½-lb cauliflower
    ½ cup (bottled) French dressing

(2) Invert cauliflower carefully into the center of a round serving platter, arrange tomato slices around it in an overlapping circle:
    4 tomatoes, peeled and sliced

(3) Pour over cauliflower and tomatoes:
    ½ cup (bottled) Italian dressing

(4) Sprinkle tomatoes with:
    ¼ cup finely chopped onion
    ¼ cup finely chopped parsley

(5) Rice over cauliflower:
    1 hard-cooked egg white
    1 hard-cooked egg yolk

(6) Garnish platter and center of cauliflower with:
    parsley sprigs

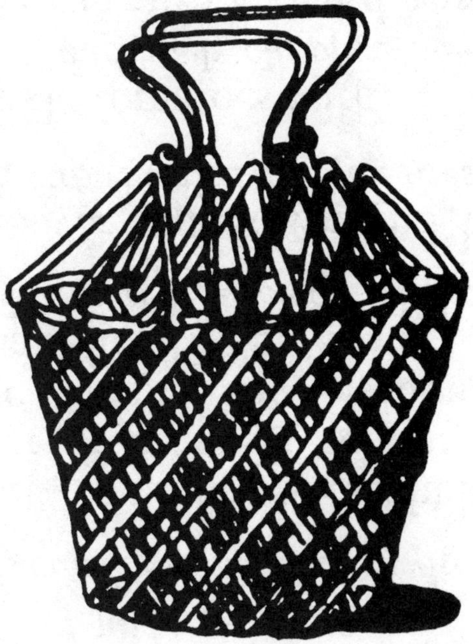

WATERCRESS AND EGG SALAD

(1) Beat well and chill:
   1 cup French Dressing I, page 88
   2 tbs chili sauce
   2 tbs freshly grated horseradish
   or minced radishes
   1 tbs minced onion

(2) Rub bowl with cut side of ½ garlic clove, discard garlic and arrange in bowl:
   2 bunches watercress, all wilted leaves
   and stems removed

(3) Pour over dressing, Step 1, and add 2 hard-cooked egg whites, riced through a coarse sieve.

COOKED CHICKEN FOR SALADS

(1) Place in a kettle of just enough boiling, salted water to cover:
1 4–5-lb roasting chicken, or 2 fryers
1 carrot, scraped and quartered
½ onion
3 sprigs parsley
1 peppercorn

(2) When water returns to a boil, skim off scum, reduce heat, cover and simmer until chicken is tender, about 45 minutes for fryers and up to 2 hours for roasting chicken. Take from heat and let chicken cool in the stock.

(3) Lift off fat, take chicken meat from bones, discard skin and store meat in the stock in refrigerator.

(4) Drain meat well and cut into large pieces just before preparing salad. Do not grind the meat. Some salads are based on cubed or diced chicken, which means cutting all meat to evenly sized dice, usually ⅜ to ½ inch.

The roasting chicken or fryers will yield about 4 cups cooked chicken, sufficient for a chicken salad for 6.

CHICKEN SALAD I

(1) Fold gently to avoid breaking chicken pieces:

4 cups cold cooked chicken, page 57
2 cups cooked green peas or other vegetable
2 cups diced celery
1¾ cups mayonnaise or Blender Mayonnaise,
page 93
salt and pepper to taste

(2) Arrange in a lettuce-lined bowl and spread top of salad with:

¼ cup mayonnaise

(3) Garnish with:

hard-cooked eggs, sliced
stuffed olives, sliced
pimento strips
chopped parsley

CHICKEN SALAD II

(1) Fold gently to avoid breaking chicken pieces:
   4 cups cold cooked chicken, page 57
   ½ cup scalded almonds
   1 tbs minced shallots
   *1–1½ cups Lemon Mayonnaise
   to taste, page 93*
   salt and pepper to taste

(2) Mound salad in the center of a serving platter. Surround it with a ring of:
   2 cups cantaloupe balls
   2 cups green seedless grapes
   *2 cups canned grapefruit sections, drained,
   or the sections of 2 sweet grapefruit*

(3) Pour over fruit salad:
   ½–⅔ cup French Dressing II, page 89

(4) Garnish chicken salad with:
   capers

(5) Garnish fruit salad with:
   chopped chervil and parsley

(6) Garnish platter with a circle of lettuce leaves.

CUCUMBER SALAD I
(PLAIN)

(1) Trim ends, peel or score with a fluted knife and slice thin with a vegetable slicer or a sharp knife:

4 medium cucumbers, chilled

(2) Layer slices in a bowl, sprinkling each half-inch layer with:

¼ tsp salt

(3) Place a small plate on cucumbers, set a heavy weight on the plate and let stand 2 hours.

(4) Drain off salt water. Use as recipes require or arrange cucumber slices in bowl and pour over:

½ cup French Dressing II, page 89
2 tbs cut chives

Serve with breaded foods, fish, shellfish and poultry or as recipes require.

CUCUMBER SALAD II
(NORWEGIAN)

Prepare cucumber as for Cucumber Salad I, Steps 1 through 3.

(4) Drain off salt water; stir cucumbers with:

½ cup sour cream, whipped with:
1 tbs minced parsley
1 tbs minced onion

(5) Arrange in a serving bowl and sprinkle with:

paprika
1 tbs cut chives

CUCUMBER SALAD III

Prepare cucumber as for Cucumber Salad I, Steps 1 through 3.

(4) Drain off salt water; stir cucumbers with:
    ½ cup sour cream, whipped with:
    1 tbs freshly grated or well-drained bottled horseradish

(5) Arrange in a serving bowl and sprinkle with:
    2 tbs cut chives

EGG SALAD WITH HAM

(1) Prepare, break into pieces and arrange in a salad bowl:
    1 head Boston lettuce

(2) Arrange attractively on the lettuce:
    6 hard-cooked eggs, sliced
    2 5-oz packages (6 slices) boiled ham cut into strips
    1 large dill pickle, diced and drained
    2 tsp chopped parsley

(3) Serve separately, pour over salad and mix at table:
    1 cup mayonnaise, beaten with:
    1 tbs lemon juice

ENDIVE AND ORANGE SALAD

(1) Trim, cut off base and discard outside leaves of:
6 stalks endive

(2) Peel down to the meat with a sharp knife and cut out sections, free of white skin and pits, of:
4 eating oranges

(3) Divide endive leaves, arranging them in one direction, on 6 salad plates. Top with overlapping rows of orange sections.

(4) Pour over the 6 portions:
½ cup French Dressing I, any variation, page 88

(5) Sprinkle generously with:
paprika to taste
2 tbs finely chopped mint leaves

ENDIVE AND CHEESE SALAD

(1) Prepare, as for Endive and Orange Salad, this page, 6 stalks endive on 6 salad plates. Add, laying the strips in the same direction as the endive:
3 slices swiss cheese, cut across into ¼-inch strips

(2) Stir and pour over endive and cheese:
½ cup (bottled) Italian dressing
2 tbs finely chopped pimento
2 tbs finely chopped parsley

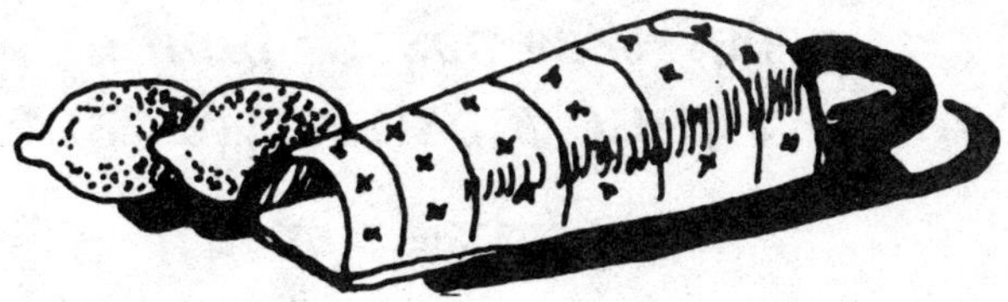

GREEN BEAN SALAD

(1) Snap off ends, tie into bunches, as asparagus, and boil, uncovered, in water to cover until just tender, about 17 minutes:

*2 pounds tender green beans**
1 tsp salt
1 pinch baking soda

(2) Drain well; marinate for 30 minutes in:
1 cup French Dressing II, page 89

(3) Arrange beans in an even log-stack on an oblong platter and pour over any remaining marinade. Sprinkle in even rows along top of beans:
1 egg yolk, riced
1 egg white, riced

3 tbs capers, drained
1 onion, chopped
¼ cup chopped parsley

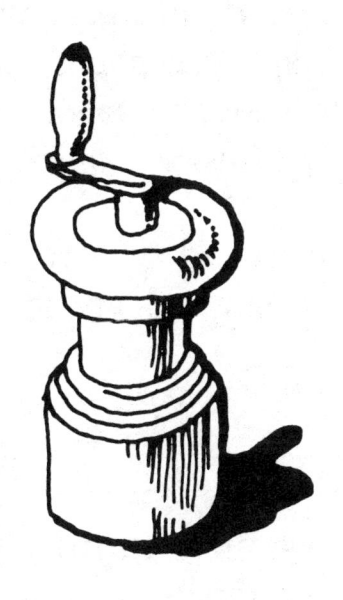

* Boil longer if beans are older.

HEARTS OF PALM SALAD

(1) Drain and cut across into ½-inch slices:
2 cans hearts of palm

(2) Line a shallow salad bowl with lettuce leaves:
2 heads Boston lettuce

(3) Combine and mound in the lettuce-lined bowl:
the sliced hearts of palm
¼ cup mayonnaise
¼ cup heavy cream
2 tbs French or Italian dressing
2 tbs minced parsley
salt and pepper to taste

(4) Rice over the salad in order listed.
1 hard-cooked egg white
1 hard-cooked egg yolk

LEEK SALAD

(1) Trim off root ends and dark-green stalks. Discard outside layer. Wash well and simmer in salted water to cover until tender, about 20 to 25 minutes; chill:
24 leeks

(2) Arrange leeks log fashion on chilled serving platter; pour over in order listed:
½ cup French Dressing II, page 89
2 hard-cooked egg whites, riced
2 hard-cooked egg yolks, riced
2 tbs minced parsley
2 tbs minced chives

(3) Serve with hot or cold meats or as a separate course.

LOBSTER SALAD I

(1) Retain meat from claws and dice remaining meat of:
    3 boiled lobsters (about 1¾ lb each);
    or use 3 lbs cooked lobster meat

(2) Marinate for 40 minutes, stirring frequently in:
    1 cup French Dressing I, page 88
    stirred with:
    1 tsp paprika
    1 tsp onion juice
    1 tsp lemon juice
    ½ tsp sugar

(3) Pour off any remaining marinade. Stir in:
    1 cup sour cream
    ½ cup mayonnaise, beaten with:
    1 tbs prepared mustard
    1 cup scraped and diced celery
    1 cup peeled and diced apple
    salt and pepper to taste

(4) Arrange salad in a lettuce-lined bowl, garnish with capers and serve very cold:
    1 head Boston lettuce
    1 tbs smallest capers, drained

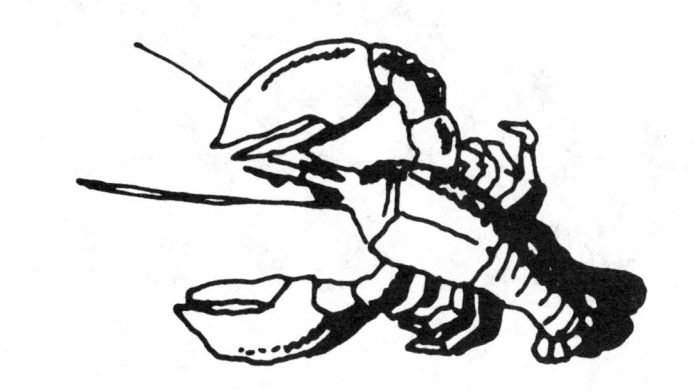

LOBSTER SALAD II

Prepare lobster meat and marinate as for Lobster Salad I, Steps 1 and 2, page 65.

(3) Pour off any remaining marinade and fold in very gently:

3 brandied peaches,* pitted and diced
½ cup heavy cream, whipped
½ cup Lemon Mayonnaise, page 93
salt and pepper to taste

(4) Fill mixture high into:

6 large avocado halves, pitted

(5) Garnish with:

2 limes, cut into wedges

* If brandied peaches are not available, substitute grapefruit sections, free of white membrane and seeds.

POTATO SALAD

(1) Boil until tender in their jackets, in salted water, about 20 minutes:
6 large or 8 medium potatoes

(2) Draw off skins and slice thin as soon as potatoes are cool enough to handle. Sprinkle with:
2 tbs tarragon vinegar, stirred with:
½ tsp salt
¼ tsp pepper

(3) Beat together and fold very carefully with potatoes until they are coated:
1 cup mayonnaise
¼ cup finely chopped onion
2 tbs minced parsley
salt and pepper to taste

(4) Arrange salad in a lettuce-lined bowl, sprinkle with capers and chill until needed:
2 tbs smallest capers, drained

RED BEAN SALAD

(1) Pour into a sieve and let drain for 30 minutes:
  2 1-lb cans red beans

(2) Pour beans into a bowl with:
  ¾ cup French dressing
  2 tbs chopped green pepper
  2 tbs chopped pimento
  2 tbs chopped parsley

(3) Chill for 2 hours; then arrange in a lettuce-lined bowl and cover surface of salad with:
  4 white onions, sliced paper thin and separated into rings

(4) Serve with a bowl of:
  French dressing

ROMAINE LETTUCE SALAD

(1) Break tender leaves into short lengths and arrange in salad bowl:
  2 heads romaine lettuce

(2) Pour over and toss just before serving:
  1 cup French Dressing II, page 89
  2 pickled beets, chopped
  1 hard-cooked egg, white and yolk riced separately
  2 tbs minced onion
  2 tbs minced parsley
  1 tbs minced chervil

SHRIMP SALAD I

(1) Cook a few at a time in salted water for 5 minutes:
   2 lbs shrimp, peeled and deveined

(2) Drain, arrange warm shrimp in a bowl and sprinkle on:
   3 tbs tarragon vinegar

(3) When shrimp are cold, stir in:
   ½ cup scraped and diced celery
   2 tomatoes, peeled, seeded and diced
   ⅔ cup mayonnaise, or to taste, whipped with:
   2 tsp minced onion
   1 tsp minced dill
   salt and pepper to taste

(4) Chill and serve salad in a bowl, in 6 half-cantaloupes or in individual cocktail glasses.

(5) Garnish with:
   lemon or lime wedges

SHRIMP SALAD II

Prepare shrimp as for Shrimp Salad I, page 69, Steps 1 and 2.

(3)   When shrimp are cold, stir in:
>   2 cups well-drained small cantaloupe balls,
>   cut with a melon-ball cutter
>   ⅔-cup Curried Mayonnaise, page 93

(4)   Fill salad into:
>   6 half-cantaloupe shells

(5)   Sprinkle with:
>   ½ cup chopped walnuts

SHRIMP SALAD III

Prepare shrimp as for Shrimp Salad I, page 69, Steps 1 and 2.

(3)   When shrimp are cold, stir in:
>   2 cucumbers, peeled and diced
>   1 tbs minced onion
>   1 tbs cut dill
>   ½ cup mayonnaise
>   2 tbs sweet pickle relish, drained
>   enough heavy cream to bind
>   salt and pepper to taste

(4)   Serve in a lettuce-lined bowl and garnish with:
>   1 head Boston lettuce
>   2 limes, sliced paper thin

ASPARAGUS AND SHRIMP SALAD

(1) Boil according to package directions, drain and chill:
   2 packages frozen asparagus spears

(2) Pour over and marinate for 1 hour:
   ½–¾ cup French Dressing II, page 89

(3) Arrange asparagus in a salad bowl and sprinkle with:
   6 slices cold smoked tongue, cut across into narrow strips

(4) Garnish salad bowl with:
   1 lb cold, peeled and cooked shrimp

(5) Serve with a separate bowl of:
   French Dressing II

SLAW WITH APPLES

(1)   Stir and chill:
1 small cabbage, shredded
2 tomatoes, peeled, seeded and diced
¼ cup broken walnut meats
¼ cup roughly chopped filberts or pecans

(2)   Fold and chill:
½ cup mayonnaise
½ cup heavy cream, whipped
salt and pepper to taste

(3)   Just before serving, combine Steps 1 and 2 and add:
2 large or 3 small apples, peeled, cored and thinly sliced

SLAW WITH BACON

(1) Shred finely and spread in a collander:
    1 lb white cabbage

(2) Bring to boil:
    8 cups water
    2 tbs salt

(3) Pour half the boiling water over the cabbage and allow to drain well. Pour over the remaining boiling water and drain.

(4) Combine and set aside:
    ¼ cup oil
    2 tbs vinegar
    1 tsp sugar
    1 tsp salt

(5) When cabbage is dry, transfer it to a salad bowl. Stir in:
    the oil and vinegar, Step 4
    1 recipe Bacon Dice,* page 74
    1 onion, diced
    salt to taste
    freshly ground pepper to taste

* Retain a little of the bacon fat and add it to the slaw to taste.

BACON DICE
(FOR POTATO AND VEGETABLE SALADS)

(1) Cut into small dice with a kitchen scissors:

> 8 slices chilled bacon

(2) Fry in a small, heavy pan over medium heat until transparent, about 3 minutes. Continue to fry, stirring with a wooden spoon until bacon is lightly browned, about 10 minutes. Pour off fat and turn bacon onto absorbent paper. Cool or use at once, as recipes require.

BACON AND LETTUCE SALAD

(1) Arrange in a deep salad bowl the crisped leaves of:

> 2 heads Boston lettuce
> 1 head romaine

(2) Sprinkle over and toss before serving:
> ½ cup Bacon Dice, this page
> ¼ cup French dressing, or to taste

BACON AND EGG SALAD

(1) Arrange in a deep salad bowl the crisped leaves of:
>   *2 heads Boston lettuce*
>   *1 head iceberg lettuce*

(2) Sprinkle over and toss before serving:
>   *⅓ cup Bacon Dice to taste,*
>   *page 74*
>   *2 hard-cooked eggs, sliced*
>   *1 tbs minced parsley*
>   *¼ cup French dressing, or to taste*

MIKADO SALAD

Prepare tomatoes as for Tomato and Curry Salad, Steps 1 and 2, page 83.

(3)   Sprinkle over the tomatoes:
⅓ cup finely chopped onion
3 tbs finely cut chives
1 tsp each, freshly minced tarragon and chervil leaves.*

(4)   Stir and pour over tomatoes:
½ cup French Dressing II, page 89
½ clove garlic, crushed

* If fresh herbs are not available, steep dried herbs in the French Dressing for 1 hour before serving.

SPINACH SALAD

(1) Discard wilted leaves and stems and shred:
    1 8-oz package washed spinach

(2) Press through a sieve and shape into marble-sized balls; then roll in chives:
    1 8-oz package cream cheese
    salt to taste
    ¼ cup finely cut chives

(3) Halve, seed and cut into balls with a melon-ball cutter:
    2 ripe cantaloupes

(4) Marinate in refrigerator for 30 minutes, stirring frequently:
    the melon balls
    ½ cup (bottled) French dressing

(5) Arrange spinach in a wide bowl and top with a mound of cheese and melon balls. Pour on:
    ¼ cup French dressing
    the chives remaining from Step 2

(6) Pass separately:
    additional French dressing

MACARONI SALAD

(1) Break into small pieces and boil in salted water according to package directions. Reduce boiling time by 2–3 minutes. Drain, cool and chill:
3 cups broken elbow macaroni

(2) Whip cream, fold into remaining ingredients and pour over macaroni:
½ cup heavy cream
½ cup (bottled) Italian dressing
2 tbs freshly grated or well drained bottled horseradish

(3) Serve salad in a bowl lined with:
1 bunch fresh watercress, trimmed and crisped

CAPRI SALAD

Prepare 1 recipe Potato Salad, page 67, Steps 1 and 2.
(3) While potatoes are still warm, pour over:
½ cup beef bouillon
½ cup French Dressing II, page 89

(4) Arrange salad in a salad bowl and completely cover it with:
3 eating apples, peeled, cored and sliced very thin
½ recipe Bacon Dice, crumbled, page 74

(5) Serve at once before apples darken.

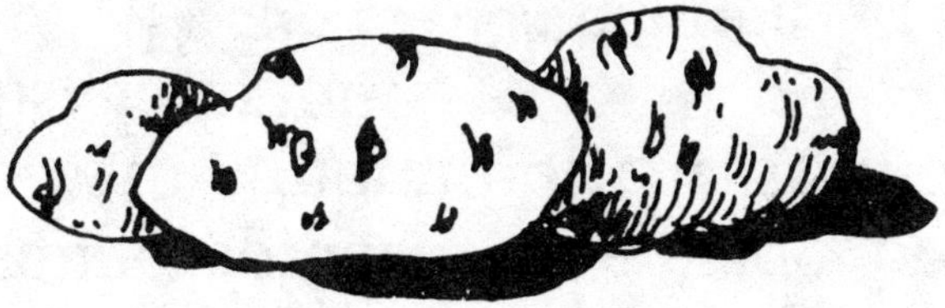

CUCUMBER AND YOGURT SALAD

(1) Peel, seed, dice, drain and chill:
5 medium cucumbers

(2) Beat and chill:
1–1½ cups yogurt, to taste
1 clove garlic, crushed
3 tbs wine vinegar
salt and pepper to taste

(3) Stir and pour into a lettuce-lined bowl:
the diced cucumbers
the yogurt dressing
8 Boston lettuce leaves

(4) Sprinkle over top of salad and serve:
½ cup chopped, salted pistachio nuts

LIMA BEAN SALAD

(1) Cook according to package directions and drain:
3 packages frozen baby lima beans

(2) While beans are still warm, beat and pour over them:
⅔ cup French Dressing II, page 89
2 tsp brown mustard
1 tbs minced onion

(3) When beans are cool, refrigerate for 1 hour. Beat until smooth and pour over them:
½ cup Green Mayonnaise, page 93
2 tbs minced parsley

(4) Mix and serve at the table.

BACON AND CHICORY SALAD

(1) Chill and cut across into 1-inch strips with kitchen scissors, set aside:
8 slices thick bacon

(2) Prepare and crisp:
*2 heads chicory
1 romaine lettuce*

(3) When bacon has reached room temperature, fry it slowly until golden, about 12 minutes. Stir with a wooden spoon to separate strips, drain on absorbent paper.

(4) Arrange in salad bowl:
*the crisp greens
½ cup Celery Seed Dressing, page 90
the drained bacon strips*

(5) Mix salad at table, add:
*2 tbs thinly sliced scallions
freshly ground black pepper to taste*

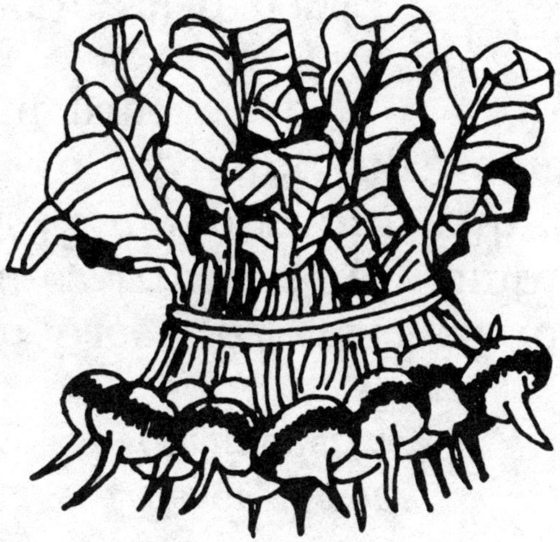

RADISH SALAD

(1) Wash, dry, trim off root ends and leaves. Cut across into thin slices:
3 bunches red radishes

(2) Sprinkle very lightly with salt and set aside for 20 minutes, drain:
salt to taste

(3) Beat and pour over radishes. Arrange in a salad bowl:
¼ cup (bottled) French dressing
½ cup mayonnaise

(4) Garnish bowl with a border of:
6 hard-cooked eggs, sliced

(5) Butter, cut into fingers and serve with salad:
4 slices white bread
4 tbs soft butter

ONION SALAD

(1) Cut across into thin, even slices:
   6 large or 8 medium onions

(2) Melt butter in a wide pan, add onion slices without breaking them. Simmer slowly until transparent, not brown, about 4 minutes. Remove slices to a shallow bowl and cool.

(3) Before they are cold, pour over and chill:
   ½–¾ cup French Dressing II, page 89

(4) Serve onion salad sprinkled with:
   ¼ cup chopped walnuts
   2 tbs minced parsley

TOMATO AND CURRY SALAD

(1) Dip into boiling water for 10 seconds, draw off skins and cut tomatoes across into ¼-inch slices, drain:
   2 lbs tomatoes, about 8

(2) Arrange slices in salad bowl, sprinkle with:
   salt to taste
   freshly ground black pepper

(3) Beat until light and smooth and pour over tomatoes:
   1 cup Curried Mayonnaise, page 93

(4) Sprinkle mayonnaise with:
   ¼ cup chopped salted peanuts

SUMMIT ANNIVERSARY SALAD

(1) Discard wilted leaves and stems and break into bite-sized pieces:
   1 8-oz package washed spinach

(2) Combine in salad bowl with:
   1 bunch crisp watercress, all stems removed

(3) Pour over:
   ⅔ cup French Dressing II, page 89
   or to taste
   1 recipe Bacon Dice, page 74

(4) Rice onto salad:
   2 hard-cooked egg whites
   2 hard-cooked egg yolks

(5) Toss before serving.

RICE SALAD

(1) Prepare according to package directions, reduce cooking time by 2 minutes, drain and chill:
  1 cup rice

(2) Add to rice and marinate for at least 1 hour:
  ⅓ cup French dressing
  3 tbs chopped parsley
  1 cucumber, peeled, seeded and diced
  1 cup cold cooked chicken, cut in large pieces

(3) Arrange a border of lettuce leaves around a salad bowl. Mound rice salad in center of bowl and surround it with an overlapping circle of tomato slices:
  1 head Boston lettuce
  5 tomatoes, peeled and sliced

(4) Sprinkle over tomatoes:
  ¼ cup chopped spring onions or onions
  ¼ cup chopped chives

(5) Serve salad, and just before mixing at the table, add:
  French dressing to taste
  ¼ cup chopped pistachio nuts

BUFFET SALAD PLATTER

For a buffet table, to accompany cold ham, turkey or beef, arrange a large salad platter on a silver tray.

(1) Center tray with a Cauliflower Salad surrounded by tomatoes, page 55.

(2) Around the central salad arrange flattened lettuce leaves, stem ends under the tomatoes:

2 heads Boston lettuce

(3) On the lettuce leaves arrange small alternating mounds of:

Cucumber Salad II, page 60
Beet Salad, page 53

(4) At both sides of the tray arrange:

Asparagus Salad, page 52, or Green Bean Salad, page 63

(5) Fill the four corners of the tray with:

1 recipe Potato Salad, page 67

TOMATO SALAD

(1) Immerse in boiling water for 10 seconds, draw off skins and slice across:
    2 lbs (about 8) ripe tomatoes

(2) Drain slices on paper towel; transfer them to a salad bowl rubbed with:
    cut side of ½ clove garlic

(3) Discard garlic. Over tomatoes sprinkle in order listed:
    ¼ cup French dressing, or to taste
    3 tbs finely chopped onion
    3 tbs finely chopped parsley
    1 hard-cooked egg white, riced
    1 hard-cooked egg yolk, riced

(4) Garnish with:
    6 paper-thin lemon slices

FRENCH DRESSING I

(1) Stir in a shallow dish and pour over salad just before serving:

½ tsp salt
⅛ tsp white pepper
4 tbs tarragon vinegar
6 tbs oil

VARIATIONS:
(1) Substitute 3 tbs lemon juice for the vinegar.
(2) Add ½ tsp minced onion.
(3) Substitute red wine for the vinegar.
(4) Add ¼ tsp dry mustard.
(5) Increase vinegar to 6 tbs for marinades and for tart salads; reduce vinegar to 3 tbs for mild salads.
(6) Rub dish with a split garlic clove before mixing dressing.
(7) Use 1½ tbs each vinegar and lemon juice instead of vinegar.

FRENCH DRESSING II

(1) Shake in jar or beat, store in refrigerator until needed and shake again before using:

> ⅔ cup vinegar
> 3 tsp salt
> 3 tsp dry mustard
> 3 tsp sugar, or to taste
> 2 tsp paprika
> ¼ tsp black pepper
> 2 cups salad oil

(2) For an emulsified, thick dressing, blend until smooth, about 14 seconds.

Use any of the variations listed under French Dressing I.

CELERY SEED DRESSING

(1) Remove 2 ice cubes from freezer tray. Return them to freezer in separate dish to bring them down to "crackling" cold.

(2) Beat with electric beater for 3 minutes at top speed:
2 tsp salt
¼ tsp freshly ground black pepper
1 tsp Dijon or prepared mustard
½ tsp sugar
2 tbs finely minced onion
1¼ cups oil
10 tbs tarragon vinegar
½ cup heavy cream

(3) Add and beat until thickened, but not until ice dissolves:
the 2 ice cubes

(4) Take out ice and beat in:
1 tbs celery seed

CHEESE DRESSING I

(1) Rice cheese and stir into a paste with:
 ½ 3-oz package cream cheese
 ½-cup French Dressing I, page 88

(2) Stir in, chill and serve over green or fruit salads:
 ½ cup additional French dressing
 ¼ cup chopped walnuts

CHEESE DRESSING II

(1) Rice cheeses and stir into a paste with:
 ½ 3-oz package cream cheese
 ½ 4-oz package Roquefort cheese
 ½-cup French Dressing I, page 88

(2) Stir in, chill and serve over green, mixed, fruit or tomato salads:
 ½ cup additional French dressing
 ¼ cup chopped pecans
 2 tbs sherry

RUSSIAN DRESSING

Shake in a jar and refrigerate at least one hour before using:

1 cup oil
1 cup tarragon vinegar
2–3 tsp salt, to taste
¼ tsp white pepper
3 tbs minced green pepper
3 tbs minced onion
3 tbs minced parsley
6 tbs chili sauce

Quantity is sufficient for 2 or 3 salads. Always shake before serving.

BLENDER MAYONNAISE

(1) Blend at medium speed for 10 seconds:
1 whole egg
1 tbs tarragon vinegar
1 tsp salt
1 tbs lemon juice
pepper to taste

VARIATIONS:

(1) *Lemon Mayonnaise.* Use all lemon juice instead of vinegar and lemon juice.
(2) *Mustard Mayonnaise.* Add 1 tbs prepared mustard per recipe of Blender Mayonnaise.
(3) *Green Mayonnaise.* Add spinach leaves, parsley, chives and chervil to taste when mayonnaise is almost completed. Blend until smooth.
(4) *Cream Mayonnaise.* Fold ¼ cup heavy cream, whipped, into 1 recipe Blender Mayonnaise.

(2) Open top and add in a thin stream:
1 cup oil

(3) Remove mayonnaise and chill in a closed container until needed.

(5) *Curried Mayonnaise.* Stir 1 tbs curry powder with 2 tbs mayonnaise until smooth. Return to blender and blend until smooth.
(6) *Onion Mayonnaise.* Add 1 tbs roughly chopped onion to blender just before completing mayonnaise.
(7) *Roquefort Mayonnaise.* Add ¼ cup crumbled Roquefort cheese to blender when mayonnaise is almost completed and blend until smooth. Add a little cream if dressing is too thick.

THOUSAND ISLAND DRESSING

Shake all ingredients in a large jar; chill until needed:

1 cup mayonnaise
8 tbs sour cream
2 tbs lime or lemon juice, or
tarragon vinegar
1 tsp celery salt, or to taste
½ tsp salt, or to taste
½ tsp chili powder
½ tsp paprika
¼ tsp pepper
2 tbs minced onion
2 tbs minced parsley
3 tbs minced stuffed olives
¼ cup minced dill pickle
¼ cup minced pimento
¼ cup minced green pepper

Add more mayonnaise to taste. Shake again before serving. Makes approximately 2 cups.

INDEX

Abjy L'Amid, 26
Ascona Minestrone, 46
Asparagus and Shrimp Salad, 71
Asparagus Salad, 52

Bacon and Chicory Salad, 81
Bacon and Egg Salad, 75
Bacon and Lettuce Salad, 74
Bacon Dice, 74
Beef Bouillon, 13
Beet Salad, 53
Black Bean Soup, 35
Blender Mayonnaise, 93
Broccoli Salad, 54
Buffet Salad Platter, 86

Capri Salad, 78
Cauliflower Salad, 55
Celery Seed Dressing, 90
Cheese Dressing I, II, 91
Chicken and Lemon Soup, 48

Chicken Salad I, 58
Chicken Salad II, 59
Chicken Stock, 16
Chilled Buttermilk Soup, 31
Chilled Carrot Soup, 44
Chilled Consommé Caruso, 47
Chilled Cucumber Cream, 28
Clam and Chicken Broth, 23
Clam and Tomato Broth, 23
Cold Consommés, 14–15
Consommé Delice, 47
Cooked Chicken for Salads, 57
Cream of Chicken Soup I, 17
Cream of Chicken Soup II, 18–19
Cream of Green Pea Soup, 32
Cream of Green Pea Soup with Egg, 49
Cream of Leek and Potato Soup, 24
Cucumber and Yogurt Salad, 79
Cucumber Salad I, II, 60
Cucumber Salad III, 61

Dumplings, 12

Egg Salad with Ham, 61
Endive and Cheese Salad, 62
Endive and Orange Salad, 62

Fish Chowder, 38
French Dressing I, 88
French Dressing II, 89
Fried Croutons, 11

Gazpacho, 29
Green Bean Salad, 63
Green Turtle Soup Sir James, 25
Gulasch Soup, 41

Hearts of Palm Salad, 64
How To Use The Book, 7

Iced Cherry Soup, 42
Iced Spinach Soup, 45

Jellied Borsch with Watercress, 28

Kolodnick, 30

Leek Salad, 64
Lentil Soup I, 36
Lentil Soup II, 37
Lima Bean Salad, 80
Lobster Salad I, 65
Lobster Salad II, 66

Macaroni Salad, 78
Madrilene Oporto, 30
Malakoff Soup, 31
Manhattan Clam Chowder, 22
Mikado Salad, 76
Mushroom Soup, 27

New England Clam Chowder, 21

Onion Salad, 83
Onion Soup, 33

Potato Salad, 67
Preparing Salad Greens, 51

Radish Salad, 82
Red Bean Salad, 68
Rice Salad, 85
Romaine Lettuce Salad, 68
Russian Dressing, 92

Salmon Chowder, 39
Senegalaise, 20
Shrimp Salad I, 69
Shrimp Salad II, III, 70

Slaw with Apples, 72
Slaw with Bacon, 73
Soup Garnishes, 9–10
Spinach Salad, 77
Stschy, 40
Summer Fruit Soup, 29
Summit Anniversary Salad, 84

Tarator, 48
Thousand Island Dressing, 94
Toasted Croutons, 11
Tomato and Curry Salad, 83
Tomato Salad, 87
Tomato Soup, 34
Turkey Soup, 43

Vichyssoise, 25

Watercress and Egg Salad, 56